THE BIG BOOK OF
REAL TRUCKS

STOCK AND GRAIN TRUCK

"JEEP" FIRE TRUCK

TRUCKS THAT PERFORM SPECIAL SERVICES

TRACTOR AND MILK-TANK TRAILER

HIGH-LIFT DUMP TRUCK

REFUSE TRUCK

POWER-WAGON TRUCK

PICK-UP TRUCK

TRACTOR AND VAN TRAILER

BOOKMOBILE TRUCK

REFRIGERATED ICE CREAM TRUCK

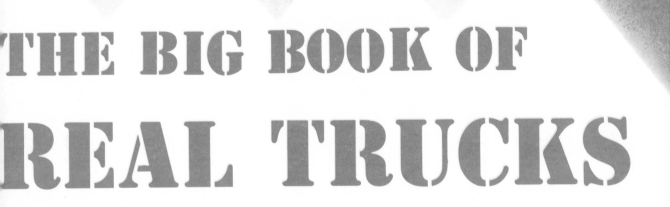

THE BIG BOOK OF
REAL TRUCKS

By GEORGE J. ZAFFO

GROSSET & DUNLAP · Publishers · NEW YORK

GOOSENECK TRAILER • The gooseneck trailer carries heavy machinery and steam shovels. Sometimes it even carries houses.

Do you see the front of the trailer? It goes over the wheels of the tractor. It is like the neck of a goose.

The gooseneck trailer and tractor has 14 wheels. It has 8 wheels
on the trailer. It has 6 wheels on the tractor.

The driver works the brakes of the trailer. He works them from
the seat of the cab. He works the lights, too.

TANK TRAILER • This truck carries gasoline. It is carried in the big tank behind the tractor. The inside of the big tank is divided into sections. This keeps the gasoline from going to one side of the truck. An even load makes it easier for the man to drive the truck.

Gasoline trucks have a chain dragging on the road. This chain sends electricity from the truck into the ground. The chain keeps sparks from setting fire to the gasoline. The word "Gasolene" on the truck is a trade name. Do you see the difference in the spelling?

EUCLID DUMP TRUCK • This dump truck can carry tons of earth or rock over very rough ground. It is used on many road-building jobs. The tires have a deep tread, like snow tires, which helps the truck move more easily in mud or soft earth.

The truck moves by Diesel power. Heavy smoke from the Diesel engine comes out of the two tall pipes above the hood, in front.

The wire blanket is used to cover rock when blasting. It protects workmen from being hit by small flying rocks.

SCENICRUISER • This streamlined bus is higher and longer than most buses. Passengers look out of the big windows. They get a good view as the bus goes along. The passengers sit on two different levels. The luggage is kept in the bottom of the bus.

The bus is air-conditioned. It is heated in cold weather. The bus rides smoothly. The seats are comfortable.

On long trips the bus stops at stations along the way. Passengers may then get out and walk around. They may get something to eat.

LOW-BED TRAILER • This special tractor-trailer is needed when a very heavy transformer, such as the one shown above, is moved. The jeep-dolly trailer in front of the low-bed trailer helps spread the weight of the load on the ground. There are fifty tires in all.

The travel route of such a trailer is always checked ahead of time for clearance, such as at turns and underpasses. A small truck leads the way and another small truck follows behind. The Diesel engine in the tractor up front uses about five gallons of fuel per mile.

1. The truck driver gets up late in the morning. He dresses and has his breakfast. Then he goes to work. He is ready to start the day.

2. He checks in. He finds which truck he is to drive. He gets his log book. He must write about his trip in the log book.

5. The truck driver stops at a toll gate. He has to pay a toll to go through. Trucks often have to pay more than passenger cars.

6. The truck driver stops to eat. He writes the time in his log book. A driver must not drive more than ten hours. This is a law.

9. If a truck stops on a road, the driver uses flare pots. These are long-burning oil lamps. The flare pots warn other cars. The driver writes the time of his stop in his log book.

DRIVER'S DAY

3. Men have greased and oiled the truck. They have filled it with gasoline. They have checked the motors. The truck is ready to go.

4. The truck driver is given a route to follow. The heavy truck travels only over strong roads and bridges. It can go only under high bridges.

7. State laws tell how much weight trucks may carry in order to go on certain roads. Drivers must stop at weighing stations.

8. The driver goes fast along a straight road where there is little traffic. He goes slower when there is heavy traffic on the road.

10. The driver stops at a relay stop. A new driver is waiting to take the truck. The new driver will drive for the next ten hours.

The driver goes to a hotel to sleep. The next morning he goes to the relay stop. He drives another truck back to his home.

REFRIGERATOR TRAILER • The inside of this trailer is kept cold by its own Diesel-powered refrigerator. Butter, eggs, meat, fish, fruit and vegetables are kept fresh as the food is sent to places hundreds of miles away. The trailer can also carry frozen foods.

A Diesel tractor pulls the trailer. See the tall exhaust pipe just behind the cab? Sometimes trucks travel very far with two drivers. The cab of the tractor in this picture has a bed just behind the driver's seat. One of the men can sleep while the other one drives.

DIESEL FREIGHT TRAILER • This trailer carries many things. Often these things, called freight, are taken to stores in another state. Freight trucks are big. They have many different state license plates on them.

The front part of the truck is called the tractor. This has the cab and the motor. The back part is called the trailer. This truck has a Diesel motor. This motor is cheaper to run than a gasoline motor.

MOVING VAN TRAILER • Trailers such as this one are used to move furniture and household things to a new home or apartment. Small things and clothes are carefully packed in boxes and sealed. Furniture is covered with a blanket before something else is put on top.

Because the wheels at the back end of the trailer are smaller than the ones up front, there is more loading space inside the van. The men load the trailer so that everything inside is snug. If this is not done, things might get damaged from bumping about.

WHAT MAKES AN ENGINE RUN?

PARTS OF A V-8 ENGINE

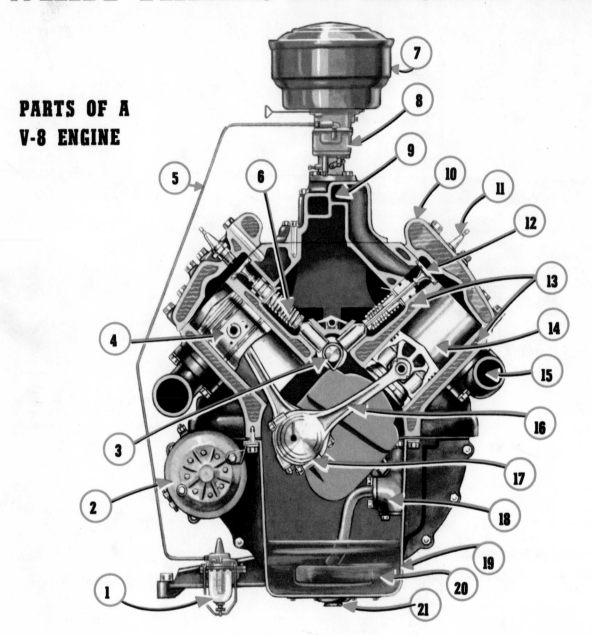

1 Fuel Pump	9 Intake Manifold	17 Crankshaft
2 Starter	10 Cylinder Head	with Connecting
3 Camshaft	11 Spark Plug	Rod Attached
4 Four-Ring Piston	12 Valve	18 Oil Pump
5 Fuel Line	13 Water Jacket	19 Crankcase
6 Valve Spring	14 Cylinder Wall	20 Oil
7 Air Filter	15 Exhaust Manifold	21 Drain Plug
8 Carburetor	16 Connecting Rod	

Can you ride a bicycle? You make it go by using your legs. They give power to the pedals. A gasoline engine runs the same way. The piston action on the crankshaft is the same as your feet pressing on the bicycle pedals.

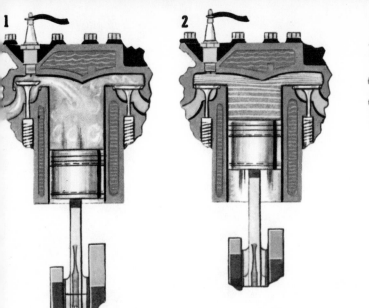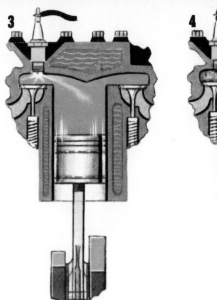

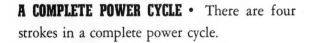

A COMPLETE POWER CYCLE • There are four strokes in a complete power cycle.

1. INTAKE STROKE • This is stroke one. It goes down. The starter turns the crankshaft. The piston takes gas vapor through the intake valve on the left.

2. COMPRESSION STROKE • This is stroke two. It goes up. The intake valve on the left closes. Then the piston starts going up. When the piston goes up, it compresses the gas vapor.

3. POWER STROKE • This is stroke three. It goes down. The spark plug is timed by the distributor. The spark ignites the compressed gas vapor. The explosion makes the piston go down. This makes the crankshaft go around.

4. EXHAUST STROKE • This is stroke four. It goes up. The burned gas vapors are pushed out of the valve to the right. The valve closes. This completes the cycle.

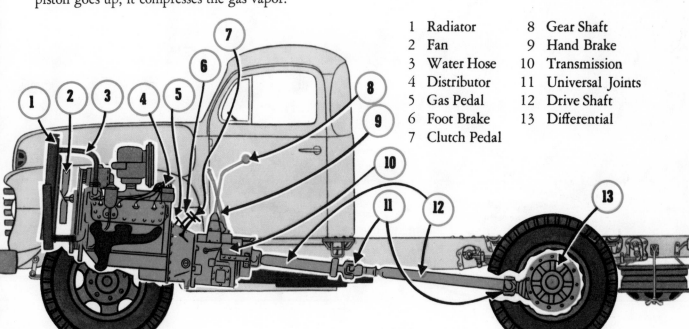

1	Radiator	8	Gear Shaft
2	Fan	9	Hand Brake
3	Water Hose	10	Transmission
4	Distributor	11	Universal Joints
5	Gas Pedal	12	Drive Shaft
6	Foot Brake	13	Differential
7	Clutch Pedal		

This is how the engine makes the truck run. First the driver starts the engine. Then the driver steps on the gas pedal.

The engine starts turning the drive shaft. The drive shaft turns the gears. This turns the rear wheels. Now the truck moves.

LUMBER TRAILER • This trailer has no floor to it. It has a long center beam, at the front and back of which are two U-shaped pieces holding the bottom logs on the trailer. Chains are placed around all of the logs when there is a full load. Then the chains are locked.

This type of trailer can also carry steel girders, metal pipes, or concrete pipes.

In this picture, the logs are being taken to a sawmill where they will be cut into boards.

AIRPORT FIRE TRUCK • The airport fire truck has a big water tank. It uses water from a hydrant, too. The truck goes to any part of the airport to put out a fire. The truck has a tank of foam. The foam is used to keep gasoline and hot metal parts from catching fire.

The turret gun is used to shoot either water or foam. The hose on the reel shoots foam in a spray.

The airport fire truck is an emergency truck. The fire truck also carries first-aid equipment.

AIRPORT REFUELER • This truck is like a gas station on wheels. It is used to refuel jets at airports. It holds 8,000 gallons of fuel.

There is a double set of wheels in front. First, there are two tires, one on each side. Then there are four tires, two on each side. When

the driver turns his steering wheel, all six of these tires turn. Usually
a regular tractor-trailer would be needed for such a heavy load, but a
trailer is hard to back up. The airport refueler is all one truck. It carries
a heavy load, and it is easily moved into place.

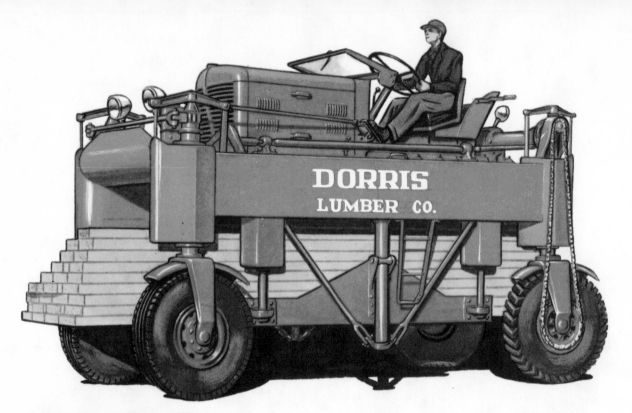

STRADDLE LUMBER TRUCK • This truck stands over, or straddles, a pile of lumber. It loads the lumber from underneath. The lumber is piled on a low platform.

The driver moves the truck over the pile. He pulls a lever. One long arm drops down on each side of the platform. These arms lift the lumber. The arms hold the lumber in place.

FLUSHING MACHINE • This truck moves along in the middle of the street. Water comes from faucets on both sides of the truck.

The water cleans the street. In warm weather, the flushing machine is sometimes used to cool the hot pavements.

HEAVY DUMP TRUCK · This truck carries big rocks. It is made of steel. It has strong braces. The front edge of the body covers the cab. This protects the cab from falling rocks.

Pumps make the body of the truck go up and down. Some dump trucks are very heavy. They cannot go on regular roads. Their heavy weight would crack the pavement.

ELGIN SWEEPER · This truck has brooms that clean the streets. It takes the place of men.

This truck can clean most places. The places that the truck cannot reach are swept by hand.

FLAT-BED TRAILER • There are no sides or back to this trailer. It has a wall at the front end to protect the driver from shifting cargo, caused by sudden stops. The cargo of rough-cut maple boards in this picture is separated into sections for easier loading and unloading.

The flat-bed trailer is used for hauling small machines such as farm tractors, small cement mixers and water pumps. It also carries concrete blocks, cut stone and wooden crates.

CONCRETE MIXER • This truck delivers concrete. It mixes the concrete while the truck is going along the road. The mixer tank is filled with sand, cement, and gravel. The mixer tank mixes them together. The mixer tank is turned by a motor.

The water tank is behind the cab. Water is run into the mixer from the water tank. It mixes with sand, cement, and gravel.

When the truck arrives at the job, the concrete is ready to be used. The driver opens the mixer. The concrete pours down the chute.

CEMENT TANK-TRAILER • This trailer is being backed up onto the scale at the cement plant. The rear wheels are put on the scale first and weighed. Then the rear tractor wheels are weighed: The tank is then filled with dry cement and another weighing takes place.

An air-compressor on the back of the trailer is used to unload the dry cement by air pressure. The pipe at the lower center of the tank-trailer is connected to a receiving line for unloading the dry cement wherever it is needed.

LIVESTOCK TRUCK • The livestock truck is used to carry cattle from farms and ranches to the market. On large ranches it carries cattle to the mountains in the spring. It brings them back to the low, warm valleys in the winter.

The sides have open spaces. There is a roof over the trailer to protect the cattle. A gate in the back opens for loading and unloading. When cattle are unloaded, the truck is backed up to a platform. The animals walk off the truck onto the platform.

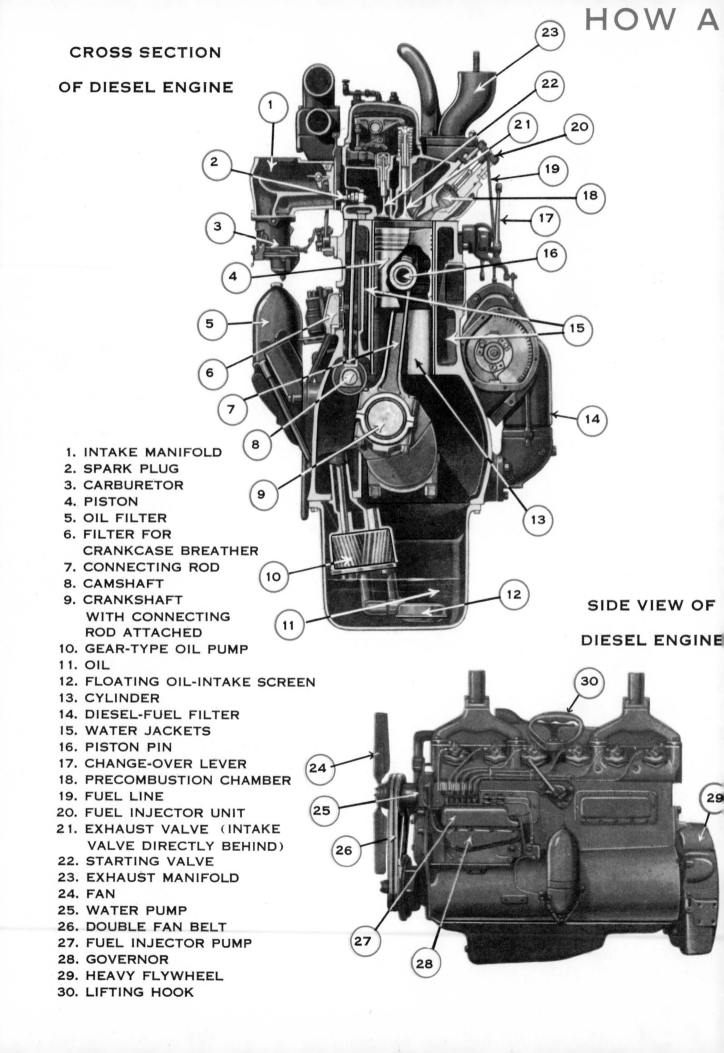

CROSS SECTION

OF DIESEL ENGINE

1. INTAKE MANIFOLD
2. SPARK PLUG
3. CARBURETOR
4. PISTON
5. OIL FILTER
6. FILTER FOR
   CRANKCASE BREATHER
7. CONNECTING ROD
8. CAMSHAFT
9. CRANKSHAFT
   WITH CONNECTING
   ROD ATTACHED
10. GEAR-TYPE OIL PUMP
11. OIL
12. FLOATING OIL-INTAKE SCREEN
13. CYLINDER
14. DIESEL-FUEL FILTER
15. WATER JACKETS
16. PISTON PIN
17. CHANGE-OVER LEVER
18. PRECOMBUSTION CHAMBER
19. FUEL LINE
20. FUEL INJECTOR UNIT
21. EXHAUST VALVE (INTAKE
    VALVE DIRECTLY BEHIND)
22. STARTING VALVE
23. EXHAUST MANIFOLD
24. FAN
25. WATER PUMP
26. DOUBLE FAN BELT
27. FUEL INJECTOR PUMP
28. GOVERNOR
29. HEAVY FLYWHEEL
30. LIFTING HOOK

SIDE VIEW OF

DIESEL ENGINE

DIESEL ENGINE RUNS

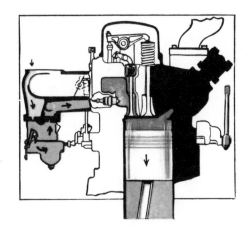

A Diesel operates on oil fired not by a spark, but by compression heat. Therefore, a cold Diesel must be started by some other power source in order to warm up the engine for Diesel fuel. Here, it is started with gasoline in the auxiliary combustion chamber (shown in black in pictures 1, 2, 3, and 4). With the change-over lever in "start" position, the Diesel part (shown in black in picture at left) is not working. After a minute, the change-over switches the engine to Diesel operation and the gasoline part stops working.

A DIESEL POWER CYCLE

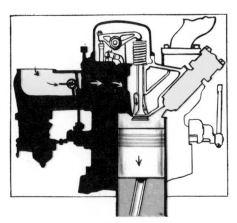

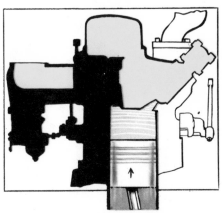

1. INTAKE STROKE • The intake valve opens and the piston goes down. In this view the intake valve (with head shown in red) is located directly behind the exhaust valve. On the intake stroke a Diesel sucks in air alone (shown in blue, above), unlike a gasoline engine, which draws in a fuel-air mixture.

2. COMPRESSION STROKE • Now all valves are closed and the piston rises, greatly compressing the air inside. The temperature of the air charge is suddenly boosted.

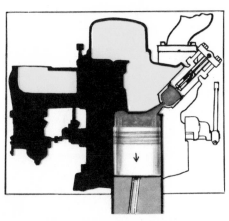

3. POWER STROKE • As the piston nears top dead center, oil is injected in a spray and is ignited by compression heat. This forces the piston down, giving power to the crankshaft.

4. EXHAUST STROKE • The exhaust valve (here shown in red) opens and the piston starts its last upstroke of the cycle, forcing the burned gases into the exhaust manifold. At the top of its stroke, the piston begins the cycle again.

SNOW PLOWS • Snow plows are used in places where the snow falls.
The plow is put on the front of the truck. It can be put up or down.
After the road is scraped, the snow plow is taken off.

The truck is loaded with snow. It is dumped in a river or on an
empty lot. The truck also carries sand. The road men throw sand on
the icy roads. This keeps the cars from skidding.

STOCK AND GRAIN TRUCK

"JEEP" FIRE TRUCK

TRUCKS THAT PERFORM SPECIAL SERVICES

TRACTOR AND MILK-TANK TRAILER

HIGH-LIFT DUMP TRUCK

REFUSE TRUCK

POWER-WAGON TRUCK

PICK-UP TRUCK

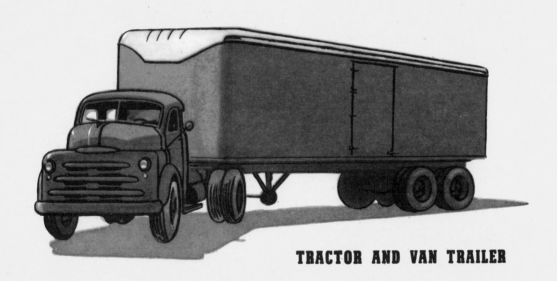

TRACTOR AND VAN TRAILER

BOOKMOBILE TRUCK

REFRIGERATED ICE CREAM TRUCK